Llamas

by Dorothy Hinshaw Patent
photographs by William Muñoz

Lerner Publications Company • Minneapolis

To Myra and Chuck
—DHP & WM

The author and photographer wish to thank Myra Ducharme, Chuck Sperry, and Jim and Deb Ellingson for their help with this book.

All photographs © William Muñoz, except: © Minneapolis Public Library, p. 7; © Wolfgang Kaehler, pp. 8, 9, 34, 36, 37, 38; © Kent and Donna Dannen, p. 13; © Bob Williamson/Visuals Unlimited, p. 24; © François Gohier/Photo Researchers, p. 30; © Michele Burgess, pp. 26, 35; © Louisa Preston/Photo Researchers, p. 39; © Jeff Vanuga, p. 40.

Lerner Publications Company
A division of Lerner Publishing Group
241 First Avenue North
Minneapolis, Minnesota 55401 U.S.A.

Website address: www.lernerbooks.com

Library of Congress Cataloging-in-Publication Data

Patent, Dorothy Hinshaw.
    Llamas / by Dorothy Hinshaw Patent ; photographs by
William Muñoz.
       p.   cm. — (Early bird nature books)
    Summary: Describes the physical characteristics, habits, and
behavior of llamas.
      ISBN: 0–8225–0067–1 (lib. bdg. : alk. paper)
      1. Llamas—Juvenile literature. [1. Llamas.] I. Muñoz,
William, ill. II. Title. III. Series.
    QL737.U54 P38 2002
    599.63'67—dc21   2001003568

Manufactured in the United States of America
1 2 3 4 5 6 – JR – 07 06 05 04 03 02

Contents

Be a Word Detective

Can you find these words as you read about the llama's life? Be a detective and try to figure out what they mean. You can turn to the glossary on page 46 for help.

camelids   domesticated   nurses

communicate   herbivores   predators

cría   herd   social

Chapter 1

Llamas are curious animals. Where do llamas live?

The Lovable Llama

Llamas are easy to love. They are calm and quiet. They are gentle. And they are curious.

Many years ago, llamas lived only in the Andes (AN-deez) Mountains. The Andes Mountains are on the continent of South America. Llamas still live in these mountains. But people keep llamas on farms in the United States and in other countries.

Llamas live in the Andes Mountains of South America.

Llamas are related to camels. Llamas and camels are part of a group of animals called camelids. Camels have humps. But llamas do not have humps.

Camels and llamas are close relatives.

These guanacos live in the Andes Mountains.

Besides llamas, three other kinds of camelids live in the Andes Mountains. The guanaco (gwuh-NAH-koh) and the vicuña (vih-KOON-yuh) are camelids who live in the wild. They do not live with people. The alpaca (al-PAK-uh) is a camelid who lives only with people.

9

Llamas reach their full size at four to six years of age.

Llamas can grow to be 5 to 6 feet tall. This is about as tall as an adult person. Llamas weigh from 250 to 400 pounds. This is heavier than five second graders.

Llamas have big, dark eyes. Their eyes have long lashes. Llamas have large ears. A llama's upper lip is split into two parts.

A llama has long, banana-shaped ears.

Llamas have both an inner coat and an outer coat of hair.

A llama's body is covered with long hair. The hair is called the llama's coat. A llama's coat has two layers. There is an inner coat and an outer coat. The inner coat has soft, fine hairs. It protects a llama from cold and from heat. The outer coat has long, thick hairs. It protects a llama from rain.

This llama has a very long coat.

A llama's coat can be many different colors. It can be black or white. It can be gray or brown. Some llamas are just one color. Other llamas have spots or patches of different colors.

This llama has two colors of hair in its coat.

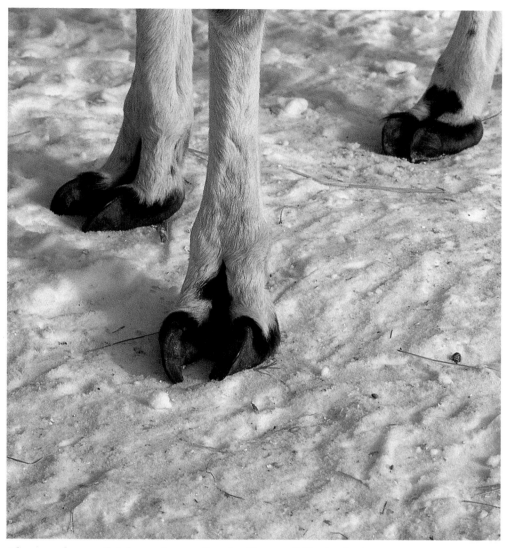

Llamas have thick pads on the bottom of their feet.
The pads help them to walk on rocky or snowy ground.

Llamas have two toes on each foot. On the bottom of each foot is a broad, thick pad.

Chapter 2

This llama is nibbling grass. What other kinds of plants do llamas eat?

The Chewing Llama

Llamas are herbivores (HUR-buh-vohrz). Herbivores are animals who eat only plants. Llamas eat grasses and low shrubs. They also eat weeds and small trees.

Llamas' teeth work well for eating plants.

Like people, llamas have upper teeth and lower teeth. But llamas have no upper teeth at the front of their mouth. Instead, they have a hard pad at the front of their mouth.

These llamas are using their back teeth to grind up food.

Llamas nip off food by pressing their bottom teeth against the pad. The teeth in the back of a llama's mouth are large and flat. Llamas use these teeth to grind up their food.

18

Llamas have a third kind of teeth. These teeth are just in front of the flat grinding teeth. In male llamas, these teeth are big and sharp. They aren't as big or sharp in female llamas. Male llamas use these pointed teeth when they fight other male llamas.

Male llamas have big, sharp teeth for fighting. Some people who own llamas remove these teeth.

The plants a llama eats are tough. So the llama spends a lot of time chewing its food. It often chews food while it rests.

Llamas spend much of their time eating. Llamas need even more food in cold weather than in warm weather.

This llama is chewing food as it rests.

A llama's stomach has three parts. After a llama chews its food, it swallows it. The food goes into the first part of its stomach. Later, the llama brings the food back up into its mouth. It chews the food some more and swallows it again. Then the food passes through the other two parts of the llama's stomach.

Chapter 3

You can see llamas with many different coats in a group as large as this one. What is a group of llamas called?

Friendly Llamas

Llamas are social (SOH-shuhl) animals. Social animals live in groups. Llamas usually live in herds. A herd is a group of llamas.

Llamas communicate with the rest of their herd.

Llamas communicate (kuh-MYOO-nuh-kayt) with each other. When llamas communicate, they talk without using words.

This llama is talking by making sounds.

Llamas make many different sounds to communicate with other llamas. Sometimes they hum to each other. If a llama senses danger, it makes an alarm call. The alarm call is a very high, loud sound. When male llamas fight, they scream or grunt.

Llamas sometimes spit at one another. Spitting is another way llamas communicate. Usually, a llama spits to warn another llama to stay away from its food. Llamas almost never spit at people.

Llamas sometimes spit at each other. Usually a llama spits at people only if it is being treated badly.

It would be difficult for a predator to attack this llama herd. Llamas can defend themselves against predators.

Living in a herd is safer than living alone. Predators (PREH-duh-turz) may try to attack a llama. Predators are animals that hunt other animals. But it is difficult for a predator to attack a herd of llamas. Llamas have ways to protect themselves. A llama can use its front legs or chest to attack a predator. And a llama's alarm call may scare a predator away.

Llamas in herds protect each other. Some llamas eat while others watch for danger.

Chapter 4

Newborn llamas are able to walk less than two hours after birth. How many babies does a mother llama have at one time?

Growing Up a Llama

A female llama usually has her first baby when she is about two and a half years old. After that, she can have one baby each year. Mother llamas usually have just one baby at a time. Baby llamas are usually born during the daytime.

Even very young llamas are alert and curious.

This very young cría is being protected by the adult llamas in its herd.

A baby llama is called a cría (KREE-uh). A cría weighs between 20 and 35 pounds when it is born. This is about as heavy as a cocker spaniel dog. A cría can stand one and a half hours after it is born. A cría's coat is soft. Its legs are long and thin. A cría nurses to get food. It nurses by drinking its mother's milk.

Mother llamas care for their crías. But all the adults in the herd help protect them.

An adult llama nurses her cría. The cría will nurse until it is six months old.

Crías love to play. They run and chase each other. Sometimes crías run in circles around their mothers.

This cría is having fun in a field.

Crías can take care of themselves when they are about six months old.

When it is about four weeks old, a cría starts nibbling on grass. When a cría is about six months old, it stops nursing. Then it can take care of itself.

Chapter 5

Llamas live and work with people in many different countries. How do llamas help people in the Andes Mountains?

Llamas and People

 Llamas are domesticated (duh-MESS-tih-kay-ted) animals. Domesticated animals are kept and cared for by people. People use domesticated animals for different things.

People who live in the Andes Mountains use llamas as pack animals. Pack animals carry heavy loads on their backs.

This llama is being used as a pack animal.

A large llama can carry over 100 pounds. That is how much two second graders weigh. Llamas can carry heavy loads for about 18 miles in one day. It is easy for llamas to walk on steep, rocky ground.

Llamas can carry heavy loads farther than people can.

People in Peru sometimes use llama hair to make clothing.

Llamas can be stubborn. If a llama is tired of carrying its load, it will lie down. It will not carry the load any farther. A llama will also lie down if its load is too heavy.

People make things from llamas' hair. They call this hair wool. People cut off the hair. They make clothing and blankets from the wool.

Llamas help people in many different ways.

People in the Andes Mountains use llamas for many other things too. They eat llama meat. They use llama fat to make candles. They use llama droppings as fuel for fires. And they use llama skin to make leather. They use the leather to make sandals.

Many llamas live on farms in places other than the Andes Mountains. People who own these farms raise llamas for their wool. They also use llamas as pack animals.

Some people in the United States use llamas as pack animals.

Coyotes sometimes attack sheep and goats.

Some people who keep herds of sheep and goats also own llamas. They use the llamas to guard their herds. Wild animals such as

40

This llama is keeping a watchful eye on a herd of sheep.

coyotes sometimes try to kill sheep and goats. Llamas protect the sheep and goats from these wild animals.

These lambs are protected by a guard llama.

A llama is extra careful when it protects lambs. Lambs are baby sheep. Sometimes a guard llama lies down with lambs that were just born. The llama protects the lambs from the cold.

The llama is handsome and friendly. It is also useful to people. No wonder the llama is popular in so many countries.

The llama is becoming more and more popular with people around the world.

On Sharing a Book

As you know, adults greatly influence a child's attitude toward reading. When a child sees you read, or when you share a book with a child, you're sending a message that reading is important. Show the child that reading a book together is important to you. Find a comfortable, quiet place. Turn off the television and limit other distractions, such as telephone calls.

Be prepared to start slowly. Take turns reading parts of this book. Stop and talk about what you're reading. Talk about the photographs. You may find that much of the shared time is spent discussing just a few pages. This discussion time is valuable for both of you, so don't move through the book too quickly. If the child begins to lose interest, stop reading. Continue sharing the book at another time. When you do pick up the book again, be sure to revisit the parts you have already read. Most importantly, enjoy the book!

Be a Vocabulary Detective
You will find a word list on page 5. Words selected for this list are important to the understanding of the topic of this book. Encourage the child to be a word detective and search for the words as you read the book together. Talk about what the words mean and how they are used in the sentence. Do any of these words have more than one meaning? You will find these words defined in a glossary on page 46.

What about Questions?
Use questions to make sure the child understands the information in this book. Here are some suggestions:

> What did this paragraph tell us? What does this picture show? What do you think we'll learn about next? Where do llamas live? What does a llama's upper lip look like? What group of animals do llamas belong to? What does a llama eat? What are a few of the ways that llamas communicate with one another? What is a baby llama called? What are two things people use llamas for? What is your favorite part of this book? Why?

If the child has questions, don't hesitate to respond with questions of your own such as: What do *you* think? Why? What is it that you don't know? If the child can't remember certain facts, turn to the index.

Introducing the Index

The index is an important learning tool. It helps readers get information quickly without searching throughout the whole book. Turn to the index on page 47. Choose an entry, such as *eating,* and ask the child to use the index to find out what foods llamas eat. Repeat this exercise with as many entries as you like. Ask the child to point out the differences between an index and a glossary. (The index helps readers find information quickly, while the glossary tells readers what words mean.)

All the World in Metric!

Although our monetary system is in metric units (based on multiples of 10), the United States is one of the few countries in the world that does not use the metric system of measurement. Here are some conversion activities you and the child can do using a calculator:

WHEN YOU KNOW:	MULTIPLY BY:	TO FIND:
miles	1.609	kilometers
feet	0.3048	meters
inches	2.54	centimeters
gallons	3.787	liters
tons	0.907	metric tons
pounds	0.454	kilograms

Activities

Arrange to visit a llama farm if there is one near you. What color are the llamas? Do the llamas live in a small herd or a big herd? Are there any crías in the herd? Do other kinds of animals live with the llamas? Ask the owners what they use the llamas for.

Go to the library and borrow a book on the Andes Mountains. What is the land in these mountains like? Why do you think the people who live there need to use llamas as pack animals?

Visit the llamas and camels in a zoo. How are these animals like one another? How are they different?

Make up a story about a llama. Be sure to include information from this book. Draw or paint pictures to illustrate your story.

Glossary

camelids: the group of animals llamas are a part of

communicate (kuh-MYOO-nuh-kayt): to exchange information

cría (KREE-uh): a baby llama

domesticated (duh-MESS-tih-kay-ted): kept and cared for by people

herbivores (HUR-buh-vohrz): animals who eat only plants

herd: a group of animals who live together

nurses: drinks mother's milk

predators (PREH-duh-turz): animals who hunt and eat other animals

social (SOH-shuhl): living in groups

Index

Pages listed in **bold** type refer to photographs.

About the Author

Dorothy Hinshaw Patent was born in Minnesota and spent most of her growing-up years in Marin County, California. She has a Ph.D. in zoology from the University of California. Dr. Patent is the author of over 100 nonfiction books for children, including *Apple Trees, Wild Turkeys,* and *Horses,* published by Lerner Publications Company, and *Dogs: The Wolf Within, Horses: Understanding Animals,* and *Cattle: Understanding Animals,* published by Carolrhoda Books, Inc. She has also co-authored gardening books and a cookbook for adults. She has two grown sons and a grandson. She lives in Missoula, Montana, with her husband, Greg.

About the Photographer

William Muñoz has worked as a nature photographer for over 20 years. You can see his pictures of animals and plants in many books for children. Some of these books are *Watchful Wolves, Ants, Apple Trees, Wild Turkeys,* and *Waiting Alligators,* published by Lerner Publications Company, and *Horses, Dogs: The Wolf Within,* and *Cattle,* published by Carolrhoda Books, Inc. William lives with his wife and son on Vancouver Island in British Columbia, Canada.